The Farewell Advice of the Prophet (ﷺ)

by

Ḥusayn al-ʿAwāyishah

Translated by

Faisal Ibn Muhammad

ISBN 1 898649 59 6

British Library Cataloguing in Publication Data.
A catalogue record for this book is available from the British Library.

Published: Al-Hidaayah Publishing and Distribution

Distributed by: Al-Hidaayah Publishing and Distribution
P.O. Box 3332
Birmingham
United Kingdom
B10 0UH

Tel: 0121 753 1889
Fax: 0121 753 2422
Website: www.al-hidaayah.co.uk
Email: mail@al-hidaayah.co.uk

Contents

Transliteration Table

Consonants,

ء	’	د	d	ض	ḍ	ك	k
ب	b	ذ	dh	ط	ṭ	ل	l
ت	t	ر	r	ظ	ẓ	م	m
ث	th	ز	z	ع	ʿ	ن	n
ج	j	س	s	غ	gh	ه	h
ح	ḥ	ش	sh	ف	f	و	w
خ	kh	ص	ṣ	ق	q	ي	y

Vowels, diphthongs, etc.

Short:	ـَ	a	ـِ	i	ـُ	u
Long:	ـَا	ā	ـِي	ī	ـُو	ū
diphthongs:			ـَيْ	ay	ـَوْ	aw

The Farewell Advice of the Prophet(ﷺ)

Introduction

Indeed, all praise is for Allāh; we praise Him, repent to Him, and seek His forgiveness and help. We seek refuge in Allāh from the evil of our own selves and of our wicked deeds. Whomsoever Allāh guides, none can lead astray; and whomsoever Allāh leads astray, none can guide. And I bear witness that none has the right to be worshipped except Allāh alone, and He has no partner; and I bear witness that our Prophet Muḥammad is His slave and Messenger.

يَٰٓأَيُّهَا ٱلَّذِينَ ءَامَنُوا۟ ٱتَّقُوا۟ ٱللَّهَ حَقَّ تُقَاتِهِۦ وَلَا تَمُوتُنَّ إِلَّا وَأَنتُم
مُّسْلِمُونَ ﴿١٠٢﴾

O you who believe! Fear Allāh (ﷻ) (by doing all that He has ordered and by abstaining from all that He has forbidden) as He should be feared. [Obey Him, be thankful to Him, and remember Him always], and die not except in the state of Islām (as Muslims) with complete submission to Allāh (ﷻ). (Qur'ān 3:102)

يَٰٓأَيُّهَا ٱلنَّاسُ ٱتَّقُوا۟ رَبَّكُمُ ٱلَّذِى خَلَقَكُم مِّن نَّفْسٍ وَٰحِدَةٍ وَخَلَقَ مِنْهَا
زَوْجَهَا وَبَثَّ مِنْهُمَا رِجَالًا كَثِيرًا وَنِسَآءً ۚ وَٱتَّقُوا۟ ٱللَّهَ ٱلَّذِى تَسَآءَلُونَ
بِهِۦ وَٱلْأَرْحَامَ ۚ إِنَّ ٱللَّهَ كَانَ عَلَيْكُمْ رَقِيبًا ﴿١﴾

O mankind be dutiful to your Lord, who created you from a single person (Adam), and from him (Adam) He created his wife [Hawwa (Eve)], and from them both He created many men and women and fear Allāh (ﷻ) through Whom you demand your mutual (rights), and (do not cut the relations of) the wombs (kinship). Surely, Allāh (ﷻ) is Ever and All Watcher over you. (Qur'ān 4:1)

يَٰٓأَيُّهَا ٱلَّذِينَ ءَامَنُوا۟ ٱتَّقُوا۟ ٱللَّهَ وَقُولُوا۟ قَوْلًا سَدِيدًا ﴿٧٠﴾ يُصْلِحْ
لَكُمْ أَعْمَٰلَكُمْ وَيَغْفِرْ لَكُمْ ذُنُوبَكُمْ ۗ وَمَن يُطِعِ ٱللَّهَ وَرَسُولَهُۥ
فَقَدْ فَازَ فَوْزًا عَظِيمًا ﴿٧١﴾

O you who believe! Keep your duty to Allāh (ﷻ) and fear Him, and speak (always) the truth. He will direct you to do righteous good deeds and will forgive you your sins. And whosoever obeys Allāh (ﷻ) and His Messenger (ﷺ) he has indeed achieved a great achievement (i.e. he will be saved from the Hell-fire and made to enter Paradise). (Qur'ān 33: 70,71)

Indeed, the most truthful speech is Allāh's Book, and the best guidance is that of Muḥammad (ﷺ). The most evil of affairs are newly invented ones (in the Religion), for every newly invented practice is an innovation (*bid'ah*), every innovation is misguidance, and every misguidance is in the Fire.

In recent times, many sincere Muslims have looked to assess the situation of our Nation, and what they saw were the effects of the Devil's accomplishments, the blackness of wicked deeds, and the blood of many wounds. They saw discord, disagreement, disunity, confusion, and anxiety. They perceived the evil results of not ruling according to Allāh's Book in the home, in the marketplace, or in society. They saw these results in schools, universities, books, newspapers, and the media; in fact, they even witnessed them in the best of places, Mosques, where innovations now flourish. And they have also seen the effects of that evil among the ranks of callers to Islām and students of knowledge.

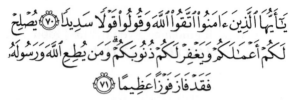

Those who hasten to do good deeds are in competition to find a cure for our Nation and its woes. The medicines, rather the panaceas, that are proffered are many, yet the situation remains unchanged – except in certain quarters, where scattered efforts are made, but not enough to effect an overall change.

If we truly want a universal cure to our woes, we must study the advice and farewell guidance given by the Prophet (ﷺ) to his Companions and to his Nation – which has been related by Al-ʿIrbāḍ ibn Sāriyah (رضي الله عنه).

The Messenger of Allāh (ﷺ) delivered a sermon that caused the hearts of his Companions (رضي الله عنهم) to quake and their eyes to shed tears. Then, at that point, he imparted to them some final advice.

That advice applies to our era as it does to all eras; it is advice that is most befitting during times of strife and discord, times when Muslims are divided into groups and parties, with each group saying, "We are upon the truth and upon what is right, and it is others who have gone astray."

Everyone is trying to show his wares to Muslims, trying to entice them to his group and away from other groups or parties. Each, explicitly or implicitly, accuses the rest of not having a comprehensive understanding of Islām, of not inviting others in a way that is pleasing to Allāh (تعالى). We live in a time when each one of us is in dire need of reflecting on the final advice of the Messenger of Allāh (ﷺ).

That need has spurred me on to write this brief treatise, in the hope that it might be received by ears that listen with compliance, hearts that are fearful of their Lord, and souls that answer the call to righteousness.

I ask Allāh (تعالى) to make my efforts in putting this work together sincere for Him, and not for anyone else. I ask Allāh (تعالى) to benefit the Muslim Nation through me, to make me a key to goodness, and a lock preventing evil. Indeed, He (تعالى) is upon all things capable.

Ḥusayn Ibn ʿAoudah al-ʿAwāyishah

After the Death of the Prophet (ﷺ)

The Messenger of Allāh (ﷺ) died: eyes shed tears, hearts saddened, the world darkened, and the believers reproached themselves for any changes that came over them afterwards. The teacher, who was beloved to all believers and who was merciful to them, died. When one loses someone who was dear and beloved and revered, his heart becomes filled with memories: there did he sit; there did he stand; he used to say and do such and such. When people lose a loved one, they naturally contemplate and relive the words and phrases that he uttered. But if the deceased was also revered as a model, they remember his advice, especially his final advice, striving with all of their soul to apply it. They reflect on his words and give them another life through action.

If your hearts were wounded by the death of your Prophet (ﷺ), then hasten to apply his final advice. ʿIrbāḍ ibn Sāriyah (رضي الله عنه) related,

وعظَنا رسول الله (ﷺ) موعظة بليغة وجِلت منها القلوب، وذرفَت منها العيون، فقلنا: يا رسول الله! كأنّها موعظةُ مودع فأوصِنا قال:

((أوصيكم بتقوى الله، والسّمع والطاعة، وإِنْ تأمّر عليكم عبد [حبشيّ] وإِنّه من يَعِشْ منكم فسيرى اختلافاً كثيراً، فعليكم بسنّتي وسُنّة الخلفاء الراشدين المهديّين، عَضُّوا عليها بالنواجذ وإِيّاكم ومُحدثات الأمور، فإِنّ كُلّ بدعة ضلالة)).

The Messenger of Allāh (ﷺ) delivered to us an eloquent and profound sermon, one that caused eyes to shed tears and hearts to quake. We said, 'O Messenger of Allāh! It is as if this is a farewell sermon!' He (ﷺ) said, 'Fear Allāh, and you must listen and obey (to those in authority), even if an Ethiopian slave is made a leader over you. Whoever from you lives after me will see much conflict; then upon you is my Sunnah and the Sunnah of the rightly-guided *Khalīfahs* after me: bite on it (i.e. my Sunnah...) with your molars[1]. And beware and stay away from innovated matters, for every innovation is misguidance.[2]

And in another narration:

فقُلنا يا رسول الله! إنّ هذه لموعظة مودّع، فماذا تعهد إلينا؟ قال: ((قد تركتكم على البيضاء، ليلُها كنهارها، لا يزيغ عنها بعدي إلا هالك، من يَعشْ منكم فسيرى اختلافاً كثيراً، فعليكم بما عرفتُم من سُنّتي وسُنّة الخلفاء الراشدين المهديّين، عَضّوا عليها بالنواجذ، وعليكم بالطاعة، وإنْ عبداً حبشياً، فإنما المؤمن كالجمل الأنِف، حيثما قيد انقاد)).

---

[1] Meaning: adhere to my Sunnah and cling to it, just as one who is clinging to something with his teeth does so with his molars, fearing that that thing will get away.

[2] Related by Abū Dāwūd in *Ṣaḥīḥ Abū Dāwūd* (3851), by Al-Tirmidhi in *Ṣaḥīḥ Sunan Al-Tirmidhī* (2157), by Ibn Mājah in *Ṣaḥīḥ Sunan Ibn Mājah* (40), as well as by others. Refer to *Ṣaḥīḥ Al-Targhīb Wa l-Tarhīb* (pg. 24) and *Kitāb Al-Sunnah* (54), by Ibn Abū ʿĀṣim, which was revised by our Shaykh al-Albānī – may Allāh have mercy on him. In the narration of Al-Nisā'ī and Al-Bayhaqī in *Al-Asmā Wa l-Ṣifāt* is the following: "And every misguidance is in the Hellfire." And that addition is with an authentic chain, as in *Al-Ajwibah Al-Nāfiʿah* (pg. 545) and *Iṣlāhal-Masājid* (pg. 11).

We said, 'O Messenger of Allāh! It is as if this is a farewell sermon! Then what do you charge us with?' He (ﷺ) said, 'I have left you upon the white [clear proof], whose night is like its day. None strays from it after me except for one who is destroyed. Whoever from you lives after me will see much conflict; then upon you is what you know from my Sunnah and the Sunnah of the rightly-guided *Khalīfahs*: bite on it (i.e. my Sunnah…) with your molars. It is upon you to obey [those in authority], even if it is an Ethiopian slave. Indeed, the believer is like an *Anif* camel (a camel that has some wood put in its nose; because of the pain it feels, it obeys the rider): wherever it is led, it goes."[3]

---

[3] *Ṣaḥīḥ Sunan Ibn Mājah* (41).

The Value of That Final Advice

Imagine the feelings of a tenderhearted mother as she says farewell to her beloved son or the emotions of a loving father as he parts from his dearly beloved child and know that the parting we are discussing here is greater and more poignant. Indeed, the Messenger of Allāh (ﷺ) was saying farewell to his Companions and to his Nation. What, pray tell, did he say to them? Did he clarify for them rulings of Islamic Jurisprudence? Did he teach them a matter related to beliefs, one that he had previously not mentioned? Or did he teach them a new ruling related to Islamic manners? The situation called for something else, for the Religion and "the favour" were complete; therefore this advice had to be the most comprehensive that he ever gave – if you will, the mother of all advice. It had to embrace all that was good and virtuous, and it had to warn against all evil.

That final advice gives you Islām, *īmān*, and *iḥsān* in compact form; it takes you out of confusion and anxiety and guides you to the way of right guidance. No wonder, for the Prophet (ﷺ) was given the ability to express much in few words. O seeker of good: let us drink from the pure springs that are his words:

"The Messenger of Allāh (ﷺ) delivered to us an eloquent and profound sermon," which was in answer to Allāh's command:

وَعِظْهُمْ وَقُل لَّهُمْ فِىٓ أَنفُسِهِمْ قَوْلًۢا بَلِيغًا ﴿٦٣﴾

But admonish them, and speak to them an effective word to reach their inner selves. (Qur'ān 4:63)

ٱدۡعُ إِلَىٰ سَبِيلِ رَبِّكَ بِٱلۡحِكۡمَةِ وَٱلۡمَوۡعِظَةِ ٱلۡحَسَنَةِۖ

Invite (mankind, O Muḥammad (ﷺ)) to the Way of your Lord with wisdom and fair preaching. (Qur'ān 16:125)

The author of *Jāmiʿ al-ʿUlūm wa l-Ḥikam* said that the caller to Allāh (ﷻ) should be eloquent, for people are prone to accepting the message of a talk when it is spoken eloquently. In Arabic, *balāghah* (eloquence) means to convey an intended meaning to the hearts of listeners in the best manner, using the most appropriate words for the task, words that attract the listener and penetrate the innermost regions of his heart. The Messenger of Allāh (ﷺ) wouldn't prolong his sermons; rather, he kept them short, yet profound in meaning.

عن جابر بن سمرة (رضي الله عنه) قال: ((كنتُ أصلّي مع رسول الله (ﷺ) فكانت صلاته قصداً، وخطبته قصداً)).

Jābir ibn Samarah (رضي الله عنه) related, "I used to pray with the Messenger of Allāh (ﷺ): his prayer was in the middle (i.e., neither long nor short) and his sermon was the same (neither long nor short)."[4]

In another narration, Abū Wā'il said, "ʿAmmār delivered a sermon to us, which was short yet profound. When he descended from the pulpit, we said, 'O Abū al-Yaqdhān! You spoke much using few words; better yet had you breathed (i.e. prolonged your sermon).'' He (رضي الله عنه) said, "Indeed, I heard the Messenger of Allāh (ﷺ) say,

إِنّ طول صلاة الرجل وقِصَر خطبته مئنّة من فقهه، فأطيلوا الصلاة واقصُروا الخطبة، وإِنّ من البيان سحراً.

[4] Muslim (866).

> 'Verily, the prolongation of a man's prayer and the brevity of his sermon are signs of his understanding (*Fiqh*); therefore prolong the prayer and shorten the *Khuṭbah* (sermon), and indeed there is magic in some kinds of speech."[5]

Once, when a man stood and delivered a long talk, 'Amr ibn Al-'Āṣ (ﷺ) said, "Had he been more moderate in his speech, it would have been better for him. I heard the Messenger of Allāh (ﷺ) say,

لقد رأيت – أو أُمِرت – أن أتجوّز في القول، فإنّ الجواز هو خير.

> 'I saw that I should – or I was ordered to – be brief in speech, for indeed, brevity is good.'"[6]

Here we are today with copious and flowery speech, yet what is our situation? And what is our status among the nations? We live in a time when orators among us are many, scholars few, a time when our words are abundant, and our actions few.

"...One that caused eyes to shed tears and hearts to quake." The tears and quaking referred to indicate a high level of *Īmān*. Allāh (ﷻ) says:

إِنَّمَا ٱلْمُؤْمِنُونَ ٱلَّذِينَ إِذَا ذُكِرَ ٱللَّهُ وَجِلَتْ قُلُوبُهُمْ

> The believers are only those who, when Allāh is mentioned, feel a fear in their hearts. (Qur'ān 8:2)

And Allāh (ﷻ) says:

وَإِذَا سَمِعُوا۟ مَآ أُنزِلَ إِلَى ٱلرَّسُولِ تَرَىٰٓ أَعْيُنَهُمْ تَفِيضُ مِنَ ٱلدَّمْعِ مِمَّا عَرَفُوا۟ مِنَ ٱلْحَقِّ

> And when they (who call themselves Christians) listen to what has been sent down to the Messenger (Muḥammad (ﷺ)), you

[5] Muslim (869).

[6] Related by Abū Dāwūd in *Ṣaḥīḥ Sunan Abū Dāwūd.*

> see their eyes overflowing with tears because of the truth they have recognised. (Qur'ān 5:83)

This is the way of the fearful, true believers:

وَيَخِرُّونَ لِلْأَذْقَانِ يَبْكُونَ وَيَزِيدُهُمْ خُشُوعًا ۩ ﴿١٠٩﴾

> And they fall down on their faces weeping and it adds to their humility. (Qur'ān 17:109)

Such are the hearts of those who benefit from advice and sermons: they know and apply, they are true in their belief, and they are repentant to their Lord.

As a result of their sensitivity, their fearfulness, their righteousness, and their tears, they themselves asked for the advice, saying, "It is as if this is a farewell sermon, so advise us." They sensed that the most beloved of people to them was bidding them farewell, which is not a point of wonder, for they were the leaders of the *Fuqahā* and Scholars to come after them. They did not settle for what they knew from previous sermons, speeches, or rulings: they wanted more, for they were insatiable in their quest for knowledge. After all the good admonitions they previously heard, they still wished to be given some comprehensive advice, which they could use to further improve their deeds and their adherence to the Prophet's Sunnah.

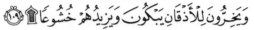

"I Order You to Fear Allāh"

Obey Allāh's commands and stay away from His prohibitions. Know that He (سبحانه وتعالى) is aware of all you do, both your open and hidden deeds. Do not let desire lead you, for it is the cause of evil and the Hellfire. Purify yourselves. Ward off the Hellfire by performing good deeds.

If the world entices you with its forbidden beauty and magic, with its shining gold, or with its deceptive pleasures, remember the Prophet's saying, "I order you to fear Allāh." If you want to be saved from trials and miseries, and if you want to be provided for with lawful sustenance, fear Allāh.

وَمَن يَتَّقِ ٱللَّهَ يَجْعَل لَّهُۥ مَخْرَجًا ﴿٢﴾ وَيَرْزُقْهُ مِنْ حَيْثُ لَا يَحْتَسِبُ

> And whosoever fears Allāh and keeps his duty to Him, He will make a way for him to get out (from every difficulty). And He will provide him from (sources) he never could imagine. (Qur'ān 65:2-3)

If you want to be saved from difficulty and if you want your affairs to be made easy for you, fear Allāh:

وَمَن يَتَّقِ ٱللَّهَ يَجْعَل لَّهُۥ مِنْ أَمْرِهِۦ يُسْرًا

> And whosoever fears Allāh and keeps his duty to Him, He will make his matter easy for him. (Qur'ān 65:4)

If you want to learn the way of success and piety, fear Allāh.

وَٱتَّقُوا۟

ٱللَّهَ ۖ وَيُعَلِّمُكُمُ ٱللَّهُ ۗ وَٱللَّهُ بِكُلِّ شَىْءٍ عَلِيمٌ ﴿٢٨٢﴾

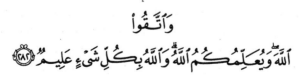

> So be afraid of Allāh; and Allāh teaches you. And Allāh is the All-Knower of each and everything. (Qur'ān 2:282)

O Muslims, if you desire to rule and lead, and if you want to be pioneers in all fields and realms, "fear Allāh."

وَعَدَ ٱللَّهُ ٱلَّذِينَ ءَامَنُوا۟ مِنكُمْ وَعَمِلُوا۟
ٱلصَّـٰلِحَـٰتِ لَيَسْتَخْلِفَنَّهُمْ فِى ٱلْأَرْضِ كَمَا ٱسْتَخْلَفَ
ٱلَّذِينَ مِن قَبْلِهِمْ وَلَيُمَكِّنَنَّ لَهُمْ دِينَهُمُ ٱلَّذِى ٱرْتَضَىٰ لَهُمْ
وَلَيُبَدِّلَنَّهُم مِّنۢ بَعْدِ خَوْفِهِمْ أَمْنًا ۚ يَعْبُدُونَنِى لَا يُشْرِكُونَ بِى
شَيْـًٔا ۚ وَمَن كَفَرَ بَعْدَ ذَٰلِكَ فَأُو۟لَـٰٓئِكَ هُمُ ٱلْفَـٰسِقُونَ ﴿٥٥﴾

> Allāh has promised those among you who believe, and do righteous good deeds, that He will certainly grant them succession to (the present rulers) in the earth, as He granted it to those before them, and that He will grant them the authority to practice their religion, that which He has chosen for them (i.e. Islām). And He will surely give them in exchange a safe security after their fear (provided) they (believers) worship Me and do not associate anything (in worship) with Me. But whoever disbelieved after this, they are the *Fāsiqūn* (rebellious and disobedient ones to Allāh). (Qur'ān 24:55)

If you desire to be the most honoured of people, then fear Allāh:

إِنَّ أَكْرَمَكُمْ عِندَ ٱللَّهِ أَتْقَىٰكُمْ

> The most honourable of you with Allāh is that (believer) who has *al-Taqwa* (piety, righteousness). (Qur'ān 49:13)

Are not boredom and wretchedness and crimes that threaten the very fabric of society from the results of a low level of *Taqwa* (piety, righteousness, the fear of Allāh)? The fear of Allāh requires from you that you accept the truth, even if it is from one who is seemingly lower than you in ancestry, gender, wealth, status, or age.

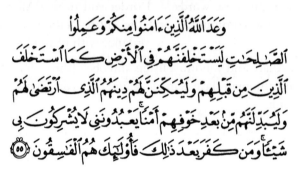

"I order you to fear Allāh" – comprehensive words that are appropriate for every time and place; appropriate for males and females, for the rich and the poor, for those who are white and those who are black; appropriate for both the shepherd and the flock. With those words – "I order you to fear Allāh" – the individual, the community, and the entire Nation can achieve success, but only if they act in accordance with its implications.

"Fear Allāh, and you must listen and obey [those in authority], even if an Ethiopian slave is made leader over you." This is similar to his saying,

اسمعوا وأطيعوا وإن استُعمِل عليكم عبدٌ حبشيّ كأنّ رأسه زبيبة.

> "Listen and obey, even if an Ethiopian slave, whose head is like a raisin, is made to govern you."[7]

And in another ḥadīth,

من رأى من أميره شيئاً يكرهه فلْيصبر، فإنّه ليس أحد يُفارق الجماعة شبراً فيموت، إلاّ مات ميتة جاهلية.

> "Whoever sees from his leader something that he dislikes, then let him be patient, for anyone who parts from the *Jamā'ah* (congregation) by the span of a hand and then dies, dies the death of ignorance."[8]

The Messenger of Allāh (ﷺ) also said,

السمع والطاعة على المرء المسلم فيما أحبّ وكره، ما لم يؤمر بمعصية، فإذا أُمِر بمعصية؛ فلا سمْع ولا طاعة.

---

[7] Al-Bukhārī (7142).

[8] Al-Bukhārī (7143).

"Listening and obeying are incumbent upon the Muslim, both in what he loves and what he hates, as long as he is not ordered to sin. If he is ordered to sin, then he should neither listen nor obey."[9]

Race or colour or outward appearance should not prevent you from accepting the truth; going contrary to this principle only leads to severe trial and conflict.

"Whoever from you lives after me will see much conflict": Here we are, living in times of conflict and disagreement – disagreement in belief, in *Fiqh*, in politics, but even more saddening, in our hearts. It used to be one group and community, now we have many groups, and each one calls to his own adopted principles. How abundant are the books on the shelves of the library, yet how abundant are the differences of opinion in them! The Muslim knows not what to accept and what to reject! And what is most disheartening is that difference and discord lead to the destruction of a nation:

وَلَا تَنَٰزَعُواْ فَتَفۡشَلُواْ وَتَذۡهَبَ رِيحُكُمۡۖ

And do not dispute (with one another) lest you lose courage and your strength depart. (Qur'ān 8:46)

The Prophet (ﷺ) said,

لا تختلفوا فإنّ من كان قبلكم اختلفوا فهلكوا.

"Do not differ among yourselves, for those who came before you differed among themselves, and then were destroyed."[10]

---

[9] Related by Al-Bukhārī (7144); one might use these narrations to argue that one must side with a certain group or bloc, but that is wrong because it only creates more discord and differences among the Muslims. And we ask Allāh (ﷻ) for guidance.

[10] Al-Bukhārī (2410).

Different nations of the world have not gathered against us because we are few in number, for we are not few in number. The Prophet (ﷺ) said,

يوشك الأمم أن تداعى عليكم، كما تداعى الأكَلة إلى قصعتها، فقال قائل: ومن قلّة نحن يومئذ؟ قال: بل أنتم يومئذٍ كثيرٌ، ولكنّكم غثاء كغثاء السيل.

ولينزعنّ الله من صدور عدّوكم المهابة منكم، وليقذفنّ الله في قلوبكم الوهن، فقال قائل: يا رسول الله وما الوهن؟ قال: حبّ الدنيا وكراهية الموت.

> The nations are about to gather upon you (inviting each other to kill you and plunder your lands), just as people who are dining call one another to their *Qis'ah* (a tray that can accommodate ten)." Someone said, "At that time, will we be few in number?" He (ﷺ) said, "Rather, you will be many at that time, but you will be like the scum of a flood (i.e., all the foam and filth that it carries). And Allāh will indeed remove from the breasts of your enemy the awe they have for you, and He (ﷻ) will indeed cast into your hearts *Wahn* (literally, weakness)." A questioner asked, "O Messenger of Allāh (ﷺ), and what is the *Wahn*?" He (ﷺ) said, "The love of the world and hatred of death."[11]

"...will see much conflict": why much conflict? It is because people will depend on the systems and laws devised by man, while they abandon what was revealed to them from their Lord (ﷻ). They will give preference to what Zayd and 'Amr say over what Allāh (ﷻ) and His Messenger (ﷺ) say.

وَلَوْ كَانَ مِنْ عِندِ غَيْرِ ٱللَّهِ لَوَجَدُوا۟ فِيهِ ٱخْتِلَٰفًا كَثِيرًا

> Had it been from other than Allāh, they would surely have found therein many contradictions. (Qur'ān 4:82)

[11] Related by Abū Dāwūd and others; refer to *al-Ṣaḥīḥah* (958).

The cause of the aforesaid strife is deviation from Allāh's Book and the Prophet's Sunnah. Whatever comes from Allāh (ﷻ) is a cause of unity and harmony, but whatever comes from other than Allāh (ﷻ) is a cause of disunity and strife.

What then is the Remedy?

"Then upon you is my Sunnah and the Sunnah of the rightly-guided *Khalīfahs* after me: bite on it (i.e. my Sunnah...) with your molars."

"Then upon you is my Sunnah": Adhere to my way, for it is light, healing, and mercy; it explains the Qur'ān and draws from its spring. How can one who takes from the Qur'ān and Sunnah go wrong when the Prophet (ﷺ) said,

تركتُ فيكم أمرين: لن تضلّوا ما تمسّكْتُم بهما: كتاب الله وسنّة رسوله.

> "I have left with you two matters; you will not go astray as long as you adhere to them: Allāh's Book and the Sunnah of His Messenger (ﷺ)."[12]

It is related that Abū al-'Āliyah said, "It is your duty to follow what they were upon in the beginning, before they became divided."

"Then upon you is my Sunnah": But how do we know what his Sunnah is? The proper way of verification must be followed to ascertain the authenticity of *aḥādīth*, and since the scholars of ḥadīth followed that way, we must follow them.

The Messenger of Allāh (ﷺ) said,

---

[12] Related by Mālik with a *mursal* chain, and by Al-Ḥākim from the ḥadīth of Ibn 'Abbās (رضي الله عنه), with a *ḥasan* (acceptable) chain, just as our Shaykh (al-Albānī) – may Allāh have mercy on him – said in *Al-Tawassul Anwā'uhu Wa-Aḥkāmuhu* (pg.13). [See *Tawassul, Its Types & Its Rulings* by Shaykh al-Albaanee, p.7 (Published by Al-Hidaayah Publishing & Distribution, Birmingham, UK)].

لا تزال طائفة من أمّتي ظاهرين على الحقّ، لا يضرُّهم من خَذَلهم، حتى يأتي أمرُ الله وهم كذلك.

> "There will continue to remain a group from my Nation victorious upon the truth; they are not harmed by those who abandon them, until Allāh's command comes (i.e., near the Day of Judgement, when He (ﷻ) will take the soul of every male and female believer), while they are still in that state."[13]

A group of Scholars hold that the people of ḥadīth are this group. Our Shaykh, al-Albānī (may Allāh have mercy on him), mentioned all those who are of this opinion in *al-Silsilah al-Ṣaḥīḥah* (1/541); they are:

1) ʿAbdullāh ibn al-Mubārak, who said regarding the previous ḥadīth, "In my view, they are the people of ḥadīth."

2) ʿAlī ibn al-Madīnī. Muḥammad ibn Ismā'īl al-Bukhārī related that ʿAlī ibn al-Madīnī said, "They are the people of ḥadīth."

3) Aḥmad ibn Ḥanbal. When asked about the meaning of the said ḥadīth, he said, "If the people of ḥadīth are not the victorious group, then I don't know who they are."

4) Aḥmad ibn Sinān al-Thiqah al-Ḥāfiẓ said, "They are the people of knowledge and the people of the narrations."

5) Muḥammad ibn Ismāʿīl al-Bukhārī. When the said ḥadīth was read to him, he said, "This is referring to the people of ḥadīth." In his *Ṣaḥīḥ*, when commenting on the ḥadīth, al-Bukhārī said, "And they are the people of knowledge." This does not contradict his other saying, for the people of knowledge are the people of ḥadīth. The more one becomes knowledgeable in ḥadīth, the more superior is he in his knowledge to one who knows less regarding ḥadīth than he does. In his book *Khalq-Afʿāl Al-ʿIbād*, Al-Bukhārī relates this verse,

---

[13] Related by Muslim (1920) and by others.

وَكَذَٰلِكَ جَعَلۡنَٰكُمۡ أُمَّةٗ وَسَطٗا لِّتَكُونُواْ
شُهَدَآءَ عَلَى ٱلنَّاسِ

Thus We have made you a just (and the best) nation, that you be witnesses over mankind. (Qur'ān 2:143)

Discussing this verse, he then said, "They are the group about whom the Prophet (ﷺ) said..." And then he mentioned the ḥadīth we are discussing here.

The Messenger of Allāh (ﷺ) left his nation upon light and guidance. The Prophet (ﷺ) said,

إِني قد تركْتكم على مِثل البيضاء: ليلها كنهارها، لا يزيغ عنها إِلا هالك.

"Indeed, I have left you upon the likeness of white (i.e. upon the clear, plain, irrefutable proof. The white night is one in which the moon appears from the beginning of it until its end), whose day is as its night: none deviates from it except for the one who is destroyed."[14]

It appears that this is an explanation of the following verse:

وَأَنَّ هَٰذَا صِرَٰطِي مُسۡتَقِيمٗا فَٱتَّبِعُوهُۖ وَلَا تَتَّبِعُواْ ٱلسُّبُلَ
فَتَفَرَّقَ بِكُمۡ عَن سَبِيلِهِۦۚ ذَٰلِكُمۡ وَصَّىٰكُم بِهِۦ لَعَلَّكُمۡ
تَتَّقُونَ ﴿١٥٣﴾

And verily, this is my Straight Path, so follow it, and follow not (other) paths, for they will separate you away from His Path. This He has ordained for you that you may become *Al-Muttaqūn* (the pious and righteous who fear Allāh much). (Qur'ān 6:153)

Jābir ibn 'Abdullāh (ﷺ) said,

---

[14] Authentic by its many chains and narrations that attest to it, as is mentioned in *Kitābal-Sunnah*, by Ibn Abū 'Āṣim (47,48,49).

كنّا جلوساً عند النبيّ (ﷺ) فخط خطّاً هكذا أمامه فقال: هذا سبيل الله عز وجل وخطّ خطّاً عن يمينه، وخطّ خطّاً عن شماله، وقال: هذه سُبُل الشيطان، ثمّ وضع يده في الخطّ الأوسط ثمّ تلا هذه الآية: ﴿وَأَنَّ هَـٰذَا صِرَاطِي مُسْتَقِيمًا فَاتَّبِعُوهُ وَلَا تَتَّبِعُوا السُّبُلَ فَتَفَرَّقَ بِكُمْ عَن سَبِيلِهِ ذَٰلِكُمْ وَصَّاكُم بِهِ لَعَلَّكُمْ تَتَّقُونَ﴾

> We were seated with the Prophet (ﷺ) when he drew a line like this in front of him and said, 'This is the path of Allāh (ﷻ).' He then drew a line to his right and a line to his left, and said, "These are the paths of the *Shayṭān* (Devil). Then, placing his hand on the middle line, he recited: "And verily, this is my Straight Path, so follow it, and follow not (other) paths, for they will separate you away from His Path. This He has ordained for you that you may become *Al-Muttaqūn* (the pious and righteous ones who fear Allāh much)"."[15]

"Then upon you is my Sunnah": He didn't say: And follow the way of such and such Shaykh or scholar or teacher, so beware of fanatically following any of the preceding; rather let us take from them that which they convey to us from the Sunnah and the truth.

"And the Sunnah of the rightly-guided *Khalīfahs*": We must understand the Sunnah just as the rightly-guided *Khalīfahs* understood it, for they were closest to the Prophet (ﷺ), purest in heart, most truthful in *īmān*, most prolific in doing good deeds, and most adhering to the way of the Prophet (ﷺ). They saw matters with their own eyes, while we hear the news thereof: "And hearing news is not like seeing it with one's own eyes."[16]

---

[15] Authentic by dint of other narrations; refer to *Kitāb al-Sunnah* by Abū 'Āṣim (16,17).

[16] Related by Aḥmad, al-Ṭabarānī, al-Khatīb, and others, with an authentic chain, as is mentioned in *Takhrīj al-'Aqīdah al-Ṭaḥāwiyyah* (401).

The Prophet (ﷺ) described them to be rightly guided; do we know anyone after the Prophet's Companions of the same description, so that we can follow him?

It is not Permissible to Depend Solely on the Qur'ān to the Exclusion of the Sunnah

It is an enormous error indeed to follow the Qur'ān alone without following the Sunnah. We can see that most deviant sects claim to be following the Qur'ān, sects that depend mainly on distortions and manifestly false interpretations.

Are the Prayer, *Zakāt* or *Ḥajj* mentioned in detail in the Qur'ān (of course the answer is no); therefore we must understand the Qur'ān in the light of the Prophet's Sunnah.[17]

The Muslim must know that the Prophet's commands and prohibitions are absolutely binding, just as Allāh's commands and prohibitions are absolutely binding.

عن المقدام بن معد يكرب قال: قال رسول الله (ﷺ): ((ألا هل عسى رجلٌ يبلغه الحديث عنّي؛ وهو متّكىء على أريكته، فيقول: بيننا وبينكم كتاب الله: فما وجدنا فيه حلالاً استحللناه، وما وجدْنا فيه حراماً حرّمناه وإنّ ما حرّم رسول الله (ﷺ) كما حرّم الله)).

---

[17] Our Shaykh – Al-Albānī (may Allāh have mercy on him) – wrote a beneficial and important treatise on the topic, called, "*Manzilatal-Sunnah Fi l-Islām Wa-bayān Annahu Lā Yustaghnā ʿAnhā bi l-Qur'ān*".

Al-Miqdām ibn Ma'ad Yakrib (ﷺ) related that the Messenger of Allāh (ﷺ) said, "Is it possible that a ḥadīth reaches a man from me while he is leaning on his *Arīkah* (a pillow, mattress, or anything similar that is used to lean upon), and he says, 'Between us and you is Allāh's Book: whatever we find in it to be *ḥalāl* (permissible), we consider it to be *ḥalal*. And whatever we find in it to be *ḥarām*, we make it *ḥarām*.' Indeed, what the Messenger of Allāh (ﷺ) forbade is the same as what Allāh forbade."[18]

This reminds us of the dialogue that took place between 'Abdullāh ibn Mas'ūd (ﷺ) and Umm Ya'qūb.

'Alqamah related, 'Abdullāh cursed *al-Wāshimāt* (those who stick needles in skin, and then fill the area with kohl or bluing, to make the skin blue or green), *al-Mutanammisāt* (those who demand others to remove or pluck the hair on their faces) and *al-Mutafallijāt* (those who demand from someone to create a gap between their two front teeth or those who do it themselves), who do it for beauty, changers of Allāh's creation.' Umm Ya'qūb said, 'What is this?' 'Abdullāh said, "Why should I not curse he whom the Messenger of Allāh (ﷺ) curses and [he who is cursed] in Allāh's Book!' She said, "By Allāh, I have read what is in between the tablets (i.e. the front and back cover of the Qur'ān) and I have not found it.' He (ﷺ) said, 'By Allāh, if you have read it, you have found it:

وَمَآ ءَاتَىٰكُمُ ٱلرَّسُولُ فَخُذُوهُ وَمَا نَهَىٰكُمْ عَنْهُ فَٱنتَهُوا۟

And whatsoever the Messenger (Muḥammad (ﷺ)) gives you, take it, and whatsoever he forbids you, abstain (from it).' (Qur'ān 59:7)

The Messenger of Allāh (ﷺ) cursed the aforesaid categories of people; our Lord (ﷻ) ordered us to follow the Prophet (ﷺ), so what

[18] Related by al-Tirmidhī, and the wording is his, *Ṣaḥīḥ Sunan al-Tirmidhī*. And Ibn Mājah, *Ṣaḥīḥ Sunan Ibn Mājah*, (12) as well as al-Dārimī and others.

he gives us, we take; what he prohibits, we stay away from; and whoever he curses, we curse. Hence the curse of those categories has its source in Allāh's Book.

We learn that to follow the Prophet's commands is to follow the commands of the Qur'ān, while to stay away from matters he forbade means to stay away from matters that the Qur'ān forbade. Whatever the Prophet (ﷺ) permitted holds the same weight as what Allāh (ﷻ) permitted, and what the Prophet (ﷺ) forbade holds the same weight as what Allāh (ﷻ) forbade. And as such, we must not differentiate between Allāh's Book and the Messenger's Sunnah.

Whoever Takes From the Companions has Indeed Taken From the Qur'ān

The Prophet's Companions took from the four *Khalīfahs* – may Allāh be pleased with them all. Of the various generations, Allāh (ﷻ) bore witness to their *Īmān* and warned us not to follow any way other than their way. He (ﷻ) says:

وَمَن يُشَاقِقِ ٱلرَّسُولَ مِنۢ بَعۡدِ مَا تَبَيَّنَ لَهُ ٱلۡهُدَىٰ وَيَتَّبِعۡ غَيۡرَ سَبِيلِ ٱلۡمُؤۡمِنِينَ نُوَلِّهِۦ مَا تَوَلَّىٰ وَنُصۡلِهِۦ جَهَنَّمَۖ وَسَآءَتۡ مَصِيرًا ﴿١١٥﴾

> And whoever contradicts and opposes the Messenger (Muḥammad (ﷺ)) after the right path has been shown clearly to him, and follows other than the believers' way, We shall keep him in the path he has chosen, and burn him in Hell – what an evil destination. (Qur'ān 4:115)

And in a ḥadīth:

ألا إنّ من قبلكم من أهل الكتاب؛ افترقوا على ثنتين وسبعين ملّة، وإنّ هذه الملّة ستفترق على ثلاث وسبعين، ثنتان وسبعون في النّار، وواحداة في الجنّة، وهي الجماعة.

> "Indeed those before you from the people of the book divided into seventy-two sects, and indeed [the followers of] this Religion will divide into seventy-three sects, seventy-two of which are in the Fire, while one is in Paradise: and it is the *Jamā'ah* (which is explained in the following narration)."[19]

In another narration, the Prophet (ﷺ) described the saved group as follows:

ما أنا عليه وأصحابي.

"That which I and my Companions are upon."[20]

Ibn 'Umar (ﷺ) related the following: "Do not curse the Companions of Muḥammad; for one of them to stand for an hour is better than the deeds performed by one of you over his lifetime."[21]

Up until now, we should notice a link: the companions took from the rightly-guided *Khalīfahs* (ﷺ) (and from the Sunnah), who followed the Sunnah, and as we have seen earlier, to follow the Sunnah is to follow the Noble Qur'ān. Hence, through this link, we can conclude that whoever takes from the Companions (ﷺ) has taken from Allāh (ﷻ); and whoever refuses the way of the Companions has indeed refused Allāh's Book, a reality that clearly points to the misguidance and deviance of those who proclaimed the Companions – with the exception of three among them – to be disbelievers (and we seek protection from Allāh!).

---

[19] Related by Abū Dāwūd, al-Dārimī, Aḥmad, and others. Refer to *al-Ṣaḥīḥah* (204).

[20] *Ḥasan* by its chains and by other narrations that attest to it; its detailed ruling is mentioned in *al-Ṣaḥīḥah* (203, 204).

[21] Related by Ibn Abū 'Āsim in *Kitābal-Sunnah*; the narrators of the chain are all trustworthy: other than Naṣīr ibn Dhu'lūq, they are the narrators of Bukhārī and Muslim. And many of the *Īmāms* have proclaimed Naṣīr to be trustworthy, not to mention the fact that many trusted narrators related from him. Our Shaykh al-Albānī – may Allāh have mercy on him – mentioned this in the book just mentioned (ḥadīth number 1006).

Those who call the Companions disbelievers are themselves the ones who do not believe in the Qur'ān and Sunnah, and are left without correct criteria to govern their lives. Those who are not on the correct path have strayed simply because they do not adhere to the way of our righteous predecessors; instead, they give their minds full reign to understand the Qur'ān and the Sunnah. And that is why groups and ideas and sects have become so numerous, with each saying, "We are upon the Qur'ān and the Sunnah." Unfortunately, they are not truthful in their claim.

Is it One Sunnah (Way) or Two?

It is one Sunnah, for the Prophet (ﷺ) said, "And bite on it (i.e., the Sunnah) with your molars." The referent of "it," therefore, must be in the singular. He (ﷺ) didn't say: bite on them, using the dual or plural; rather he said, "it," which indicates the singular, confirming that it is one Sunnah. To follow the Sunnah of the rightly-guided *Khalīfahs* means to follow the Sunnah of the Prophet (ﷺ) because their Sunnah was none other than the Prophet's Sunnah.

Of course "bite on it" is a figure of speech, which refers to strict adherence of the Sunnah, as well as to the fact that it is a way that is worthy to be followed. The only way to success, then, is in following the way of the Prophet (ﷺ) and the way of the rightly-guided *Khalīfahs*, especially considering the great number of ways that are out there and that are followed by people who are led by their desires and lusts.

One must work harder to adhere to the Sunnah – from fear of its being lost – than a Desert Arab does in seeking out his food and drink, because the latter two provide life for the body, while the former provides life for the heart.

"And beware and stay away from innovated matters": The Prophet (ﷺ) did not stop at ordering us to follow his Sunnah and the Sunnah of the rightly-guided *Khalīfahs*; instead, he (ﷺ) also forbade us from innovated matters. People might not realise that by bringing innovations to life, they are in effect removing the Sunnah: each innovation causes a Sunnah to die (And we seek refuge in Allāh!).

The word "innovation" suggests something that is new and novel, and people find pleasing all that is new. As for pleasure in the Religion, it is achieved by following what is old, a meaning that is expressed by the following words of Ibn Mas'ūd (ﷺ): "Follow and do not innovate, for you have been given what is sufficient: upon you is to follow the long-established matter."

It is authentically related from Ibn Mas'ūd (ﷺ) – in a narration that can correctly be ascribed to the Prophet (ﷺ):

كيف أنتم إذا لَبِسَتْكُم فتنةٌ؛ يَهْرَم فيها الكبير، ويربو فيها الصغير، ويتّخذُها الناس سنّة، إذا تُرِك منها شيء قيل: تُركت السّنّةَ؟، قالوا: و متى ذاك؟ قال: إذا ذهبت عُلماؤكم، وكثُرت قُرّاؤكم، وقَلّت فقهاؤكم، وكثُرت أُمراؤكم، وقلّت أُمناؤكم، والتُمِستِ الدُّنيا بعمل الآخرة، وتُفُقِّه لغير الدين.

> "How will you be when you will be enveloped by a trial, [through which] the old will reach senility and the young will grow. People will take it to be a Sunnah, and if any part of it is left, it will be said, 'has a Sunnah been left?" They asked, "And when is that?" He said, "When your scholars are gone; when your reciters will increase in number; when your *Fuqahā* will be few in number; when the number of rulers increases; when the trustwrothy ones will be few; when the world is sought through the actions of the Hereafter; and when knowledge of the Religion is sought, but not for the Religion."[22]

May Allāh be pleased with Ḥudhayfah (ﷺ), the secret holder of the Messenger of Allāh (ﷺ). He (ﷺ) said, "Do not perform any act of worship that was not performed by the Companions of the Messenger of Allāh (ﷺ)."

---

[22] Related by *al-Dārimī* (1/64), with two chains, one of which is authentic, and the other of which is *ḥasan* (acceptable); by Ḥākim (4/514), and by others, as has been related by our Shaykh, al-Albānī (may Allāh have mercy on him) in *Qiyām Ramaḍān*.

And may Allāh (ﷻ) have mercy on the eminent *Tāb'ī*, Ḥassān ibn 'Aṭiyyah Al-Muḥāribī, who said, "Whenever a people have introduced an innovation in their Religion, Allāh (ﷻ) removed from their Sunnah that which was similar to it, and then will not return it (i.e., the Sunnah) to them until the Day of Judgement."[23]

---

[23] Related by Al-Dārimī with an authentic chain, as our Shaykh al-Albānī – may Allāh have mercy on him – said in *al-Mishkāt* (188). And he said, "It has also been related from the saying of Abū Hurayrah (ﷺ), which was related by Abū al-'Abbās al-Aṣam in his ḥadīth."

At Times When Muslims Disagree about Many Matters, What Should our Attitude be Regarding Innovations?

Many pseudo-scholars and those of their ilk say, "Leave this matter, for the time is not right now." Indeed, many of them say, "Talk about innovations divides the ranks of the Muslims."

Yet the Messenger of Allāh (ﷺ) taught us differently: that if we are afflicted with much discord and division, we must avoid innovations. He (ﷺ) said, "Indeed he among you who lives (after me) will see much discord..." until he (ﷺ) said, "And beware of newly innovated matters." When we consider the disparity between what the aforesaid group say regarding this issue and what the Prophet (ﷺ) says, we have to remember that it is not permissible to make *ijtihād* (to put forth one's opinion after reflection) when that *ijtihād* contradicts a clear verse of the Qur'ān or saying of the Prophet (ﷺ).

Do not forget, then, that the Prophet's command regarding innovations is from the most important of commands that he gave to his Nation.

Next, we must remember that innovations appear in many shapes and colours – there are innovations in beliefs, in *tawḥīd* (islamic monotheism), in worship, and in dealings. Which innovations should we turn a blind eye to – to innovations in beliefs? How can that be, when we know that purity in belief is of paramount importance and is given precedence over all other matters. We fought the disbelievers and the atheists only because of the emptiness and falseness of their beliefs. Well then, what about innovations in worship? The Prophet (ﷺ) removed any possibility of doubt regarding this category and regarding all categories of innovations when he (ﷺ) said,

وكلّ بدعة ضلالة.

"And every innovation is misguidance!"

And we cannot possibly unite the Nation upon misguidance, for the Messenger of Allāh (ﷺ) said,

إنّ الله قد أجار أمّتي من أن تجتمع على ضلالة.

"Indeed, Allāh (ﷻ) protected my Nation from uniting upon misguidance."[24]

When people do not follow Allāh's commands, they bring upon themselves Allāh's anger. Imagine a soldier who disobeys a senior officer who is not only strong, but abhors disobedience as well; that senior officer would severely castigate his inferior. Now imagine us disobeying Allāh (ﷻ) and then desiring from Him His Pleasure, Mercy, and Help!

It is neither morally nor practically feasible for us to allow rampant innovations to permeate our ranks and at the same time hope for unity among Muslims and strength in our Nation. Allāh (ﷻ) says:

إِنَّ ٱللَّهَ لَا يُغَيِّرُ مَا بِقَوْمٍ حَتَّىٰ يُغَيِّرُوا۟ مَا بِأَنفُسِهِمْ

[24] *Ḥasan*, by its various chains; related by Ibn Abū ʿĀṣim in *al-Sunnah* in chain numbers, 82, 83, and 84 (the copy that contains the comments of our Shaykh – may Allāh have mercy on him); in *al-Tirmidhī*; and in other sources. Refer to *al-Ṣaḥīḥah* (1331) and *al-Ḍaʿīfah*, in the comments of ḥadīth number 1510).

> Verily! Allāh will not change the condition of a people as long as they do not change what is in their own selves. (Qur'ān 13: 11)

As we have discussed earlier, the very presence of innovations causes the extinction of many *Sunan* (plural of Sunnah). In the absence of the Prophet's *Sunan* and in the presence of innovations, can any sane person expect Muslims to unite!

"For Every Innovation is Misguidance"

The Messenger of Allāh (ﷺ) clarifies that newly introduced matters and innovations are paths of misguidance. By abandoning the Sunnah, we imitate the Children of Israel, who became destroyed when they took to stories, abandoning the application of their Religion. It is mentioned in a ḥadīth,

إِنّ بني إِسرائيل لما هَلكوا قصّوا.

> "Verily, when the children of Israel were destroyed, they resorted to telling stories."[25]

---

[25] Related by al-Ṭabarānī, in *al-Muʿjim al-Kabīr*; Abū Nuʿaym, in *al-Ḥilyah*; and others. It is also mentioned in *Al-Ṣaḥīḥah* (1681). In *Nihāyah*, it is mentioned, "Meaning, they trusted upon speech and abandoned action, and that was the cause of their destruction, or the opposite: when they were destroyed because of abandoning action, they resorted to stories."

Our Shaykh – may Allāh have mercy on him – said, "It is plausible to say that the cause of their destruction was the importance they gave to their sermonizers and to their stories, instead of concentrating on *Fiqh* and beneficial knowledge, knowledge through which they should have acquainted themselves with their Religion...When that happened, they became destroyed, a predicament that many sermonizers today are afflicted with, for most of their admonitions are taken from the narrations of the Children of Israel or from the *Sūfīs* – and we ask Allāh (ﷻ) for safety."

A Refutation of Those Who Classify Innovations into Two Categories: Good Innovations and Evil Ones

Some say that there is the good innovation and then there is the evil innovation.[26] Say, if it pleases you, "A good *bid' ah* and a wicked *bid' ah*," but remember this: the Messenger of Allāh (ﷺ) said,

[26] One might argue in favour of that statement based on what 'Umar (رضي الله عنه) said: "Blessed is this innovation." He (رضي الله عنه) said this in a narration related by 'Abdūr-Raḥmān ibn 'Abdul-Qārī, who said, "During one of the nights of *Ramaḍān*, I went with 'Umar ibn al-Khaṭṭāb (رضي الله عنه) to the Mosque, where people were scattered in groups: men praying by themselves and other men praying in groups, each group consisting of less than ten worshippers.

When 'Umar (رضي الله عنه) saw that, he (رضي الله عنه) said, "Indeed, I feel that it would be better if I were to gather all of these upon one reciter (i.e., one Imām)." He then became determined to do that and gathered them behind Ubay ibn Ka'ab (رضي الله عنه). 'Abdūr-Raḥmān continued to say, "When I went out with him on another night, [we saw that] the people were praying behind one reciter (i.e., *Imām*), and 'Umar (رضي الله عنه) said, "Blessed is this innovation (*Bid' ah*)..."

All that 'Umar (رضي الله عنه) meant by *bid' ah* (innovation) is the linguistic meaning, which signifies the new and the novel, that which is not previously known.

The following is the gist of what the author of *Jāmi' al-' Ulūm Wa l-Ḥikam* said: When some of our pious predecessors evinced approval of some *bid' ah* (innovations), it was of innovations in the linguistic sense and not innovations in the meaning signified in the *Sharī' ah*. One such example is what 'Umar (رضي الله عنه) said during the late-night *Ramaḍān* prayers: "Blessed is this innovation."

What he (ﷺ) meant is that that specific action was not performed in that specific manner prior to that time; however, it had its roots in the *Sharī'ah*. For example, the Prophet (ﷺ) would exhort Muslims to stand and pray the late-night *Ramaḍān* prayer. Even during the Prophet's lifetime, people would stand in groups as well as alone, and the Prophet (ﷺ) himself led his Companions in the late-night *Ramaḍān* prayer on more than one occasion. It is true that he later refused to do so, but he explained why he stopped: he feared that it would be made compulsory upon them and that they would be incapable of complying. Because the late-night prayer could only be made obligatory during the life of the Prophet (ﷺ), there was later on – during 'Umar's caliphate – no reason to fear what the Prophet (ﷺ) feared. We must also remember that the Prophet (ﷺ) ordered us to follow the Sunnah of the rightly-guided *Khalīfahs*, and the late-night prayer in one congregation became a Sunnah of the rightly-guided *Khalīfahs*, for the people gathered upon that Sunnah during the period of 'Umar (ﷺ), 'Uthmān (ﷺ), and 'Alī (ﷺ).

Our Shaykh, Al-Albānī – may Allāh have mercy on him – said in *Ṣalātal-Tarāwīḥ* (pg. 43), "'Umar's saying, 'Blessed is this *Bid'ah* (innovation),' is not intended for *bid'ah* according to its meaning in the *Sharī'ah*: to introduce a matter in the religion without precedent. As it is known that 'Umar (ﷺ) did not introduce something new, but rather revived more than one Sunnah, we know that by *bid'ah*, he was referring to one of its linguistic meanings: a new and novel matter that was not known prior to its coming into existence. There is no doubt that the late-night *Ramaḍān* prayer (*Tarāwīḥ* prayer) behind a single *Imām* was neither known nor applied during the caliphate of Abū Bakr (ﷺ) and half of the caliphate of 'Umar (ﷺ); it is in that sense, then, new. But from the viewpoint that it is in harmony with what the Prophet (ﷺ) did, it is a Sunnah, not a *bid'ah*, which is the only reason why it is described as being good. And that has been the explanation given by many eminent scholars regarding the saying of 'Umar (ﷺ). 'Abdul-Wahhāb al-Subkī, in *Ishrāq al-Maṣābīh*...said that Ibn 'Abdul-Barr said, 'Umar (ﷺ) did not establish this as a Sunnah for any other reason than that the Messenger of Allāh (ﷺ) established it as a Sunnah, loved it, was pleased with it, and did not refrain from consistently performing it for any reason other than his fear of it being made obligatory upon his Nation. He (ﷺ) was compassionate and merciful to his nation. When 'Umar (ﷺ) learned that from the Messenger of Allāh (ﷺ) – with his knowledge that obligatory acts cannot be added to nor decreased after the Prophet's death – he revived the Prophet's Sunnah regarding the late-night prayer in the year 14 H, a blessing that Allāh favoured 'Umar (ﷺ) with, and one that He didn't inspire Abū Bakr (ﷺ) to do, even though he was, in general, better and more keen in hastening to do good deeds than 'Umar (ﷺ). Each of the two had certain merits that were specific to him and that might have been absent in the other." Al-Subkī also said, "If it were not correct, it would have been a *bid'ah* as are the good deeds that are promoted for the middle night of Sha'bān or for the first Friday of Rajab, in which case it would have been necessary to repudiate the act of gathering together for the *Tarawīḥ* prayer..."

In his *Fatwa*, the eminent scholar Ibn Ḥajr al-Haytamī said, "Removing the Jews and Christians from the Arabian Peninsula and fighting the Turks...were not *bid'ah* practices, even if these were not done during his (the Prophet (ﷺ)) lifetime. And when 'Umar (ﷺ) said, "Blessed is this innovation," he meant *bid'ah* in its original sense in the Arabic language. In the same sense *bid'ah* is used according to its linguistic meaning in the following verse: "I am not a (*bid'an*) a new thing among Messengers (of Allāh) (i.e., I am not the first Messenger)" (Qur'ān 46:9). Both of the previous examples are *bid'ah* in the linguistic sense, for *bid'ah* according to its meaning in the *Sharī'ah* is misguidance. So when scholars refer to the good and evil *bid'ah*, they have classified *bid'ah* according to its original meaning in the Arabic language. And when they say that every *bid'ah* is misguidance, they are referring to that which the *Sharī'ah* intends by the word *bid'ah*. Do you not see that the Companions and the *Tābi'ūn* renounced the call to prayer that was performed for prayers other than the five daily prayers – for example, the two 'Eid prayers, even though there is no prohibition regarding that practice. And they disliked for the two *Shami'ain* corners of the Ka'bah to be embraced after the Sa'y between Ṣafā and Marwā...Likewise, if the Prophet (ﷺ) abstained from an action for a reason, then to abstain from it is Sunnah, and to perform it is *bid'ah*. When we said, 'for a reason,' that excludes removing the Jews and gathering the Qur'ān in one book. Also, the Prophet (ﷺ) abstained from uniting people for the *Tarawīh* prayer for a reason, and when that reason no longer applied, it was correct for 'Umar (ﷺ) to then unite them for the prayer..."

فإنّ كل بدعة ضلالة، وكلّ ضلالة في النّار.

> "Indeed, every *bid'ah* is misguidance, and every misguidance is in the Hellfire."

Both the good and wicked *bid'ah* that you might mention come under the universal, "every," which the Messenger of Allāh (ﷺ) mentioned. It is related that Ibn 'Umar (رضي الله عنه) said, "Every innovation is misguidance, even if people deem any given one to be good."[27]

When one says that this is not the time to forbid innovations and that it is better to fight deviant sects, he is wrong – for a number of reasons:

1) By not preventing innovations, they will not only spread, but will also increase in number; furthermore, many *Sunans* will become eradicated. This will lead to a dangerous spread of deviance and error, because, we must remember, every innovation is misguidance.

2) Every Muslim is responsible, insofar as he is able, to prevent and forbid evil. If one sees an evil deed being perpetrated before his eyes, he must forbid it, no matter how small that evil is when compared to other greater evils that are prevalent – such as communism, masonry, and all other false creeds. Likewise, the existence of deviant sects must not prevent students of knowledge from reminding people about the prohibition of undutifulness to one's parents, lying, usury, and all other evil deeds.

3) Lack of knowledge in society, coupled with innovations, causes the formation and spread of deviant sects. But the

---

[27] This narration has an authentic chain, as is mentioned in *Iṣlāh al-Masājid* (pg. 13), written by our Shaykh, Al-Albānī – may Allāh have mercy on him.

Companions, who constituted a society opposite of that just described, were furthest from innovations; indeed, they constituted the purest of societies, one that was free from the presence of deviant sects.[28]

4) Next, suppose that we are thoroughly acquainted with the beliefs of various deviant groups – what, then, must we do? The answer, of course, is that we need to clarify their deviance, but that will require from us knowledge, *fiqh*, and guidance. Moreover, that knowledge must be correct and authentic because emotions and zeal are not enough to refute the deviants and the misguided. One who has an understanding of the Religion is best equipped to clarify the deviation of the misguided sects, and he is best able to gather the Muslims upon what is correct, in terms of beliefs, *fiqh*, and behaviour.

---

[28] However, during their era, there did exist polytheism, *shirk*, disbelief, and wickedness. Yet, Allāh (ﷻ) helped the believers to be victorious, through the sword and spear as well as through proof and evidence.

The Danger of *Bid'ah* (Innovation)

عن عائشة (رضي الله عنها) قال (ﷺ): من أحدَث في أمرنا هذا ما ليس منه فهو ردٌّ

'Ā'isha (رضي الله عنها) related that the Prophet (ﷺ) said, "Whoever introduces into this matter of ours that which is not from it, then it is rejected."[29]

And in the narration of Muslim,

من عمل عملاً ليس عليه أمرنا فهو ردٌّ

"Whoever does a deed that is not upon our affair, then it is rejected."[30]

It is an ultimately dangerous practice to seek closeness to Allāh (ﷻ) without following the Qur'ān, the Sunnah, and the way of our pious predecessors. Also, not following them shows temerity, rashness, and transgression against Allāh's set limits.

If one's conscious allows him to steal a single dollar or ten dollars, he will have no qualms about stealing thousands of dollars. Similar is the case of the innovator: when he is satisfied with swerving from the Prophet's Sunnah, all the while being pleased with an innovation, the greater innovations – perhaps even *shirk* (associating partners with Allāh) will also become easy for him. That first step to accepting deviance and innovation makes easy all further steps that lead to every form of misguidance. Such

---

[29] Related by al-Bukhārī (2697) and Muslim (1718).

[30] Muslim (1718).

was the case with the people of Noah (ﷺ), who took the statues of certain righteous men as gods after those men died. In the beginning, when they had only recently died, the *Shayṭān* enticed the people to build statues after them, in order to remember them and emulate them in their noble deeds. Then, after the passing of generations, when people had forgotten the original purpose of the statues, the *Shayṭān* suggested to them that they should worship the statues instead of Allāh (ﷻ), deceiving them with the false claim that it was their fathers who used to worship them. Ibn ʿAbbās (رضي الله عنه) said,

> The idols from the people of Noah (ﷺ) descended among the Arabs afterwards. As for Wudd (a name of one of the idols), he belonged to Kalb in Dawmat al-Jandal; Suwā' belonged to Hudhayl; Yaghūth belonged to Murād; Thamma belonged to Banī Ghatīf in Jurf, with Saba; Yaʿūq belonged to Ḥamdān; and Naṣr belonged to Humayr, to the clan of Kilā'. They (the idols) are names of righteous men from the people of Noah (ﷺ). When they died, the *Shayṭān* inspired their people to erect statues of them in the gathering they used to sit in, and they named them by their names. They built the statues but did not worship them. When this generation perished and when knowledge became extinct, the statues were taken as objects of worship."[31]

That was how *Shayṭān* gradually allured them, first to innovate, and then to *shirk* and disbelief. Had they cut off the link between them and *Shayṭān* from the beginning, had they nipped the problem in its bud, they would not have fallen so deeply into wretchedness and disbelief.

---

[31] Related by al-Bukhārī (4920), and al-Ḥāfiẓ mentioned that this narration is disconnected, though the ḥadīth is authentic because of other strengthening chains from Ibn ʿAbbās and witnessed by his student, ʿIkrimah in *Tafsīr al-Ṭabarī*. Our Shaykh (may Allāh have mercy on him) informed us as such, and he placed this information in his second reviewed edition of "*Taḥdhīr al-Masājid Fittikhādh al-Qubūr Masājid*."

The same unfortunately happened to groups from our Nation; one example is the group who were sitting in gatherings in the Mosque. For each gathering there was a leader, and each participant had pebbles in his hand. The leader would say, "Say *Takbīr* (i.e., *Allāhuakbar*, Allāh is the greatest) 100 times, and everyone present would say it 100 times. They would continue to do the same for the *Tahlīl* (i.e., saying, none has the right to be worshipped but Allāh) and for the *Tasbīḥ* (i.e., saying, how perfect Allāh is!). 'Abdullāh ibn Mas'ūd (ﷺ) strongly condemned them for their practice.

In an authentic narration, al-Ḥakam ibn al-Mubārak related from 'Umar ibn Yaḥyā, who said, "I heard my father relate that his father said,

> We used to sit at the door of 'Abdullāh ibn Mas'ūd (ﷺ) before the Morning Prayer, and when he would come out, we would walk with him to the Mosque. One morning, Abū Mūsa al-Ash'ari (ﷺ) came to us and said, 'Did Abū 'Abdur-Raḥmān ('Abdullāh ibn Mas'ūd (ﷺ)) come out to you yet?' We said, 'No,' and so Abū Mūsa (ﷺ) sat with us until he came out. When he came out, Abū Mūsa (ﷺ) said, 'O Abū 'Abdur-Raḥmān! I have just seen a matter in the Mosque which I repudiated, yet – *alḥamdulillāh* – all I saw was goodness.' 'Abdullāh ibn Mas'ūd (ﷺ) asked, 'And what was that?' He answered, 'If you live [for the next little while], you shall see it. I saw groups in circles, sitting and waiting for the Prayer. In each circle there was a man (the leader), and they all had pebbles in their hands. The man would say: make *Takbīr* 100 times, and they would make *Takbīr* 100 times. Then he would say: make *Tahlīl* 100 times, and they would make *Tahlīl* 100 times. And then he would say: make *Tasbīḥ* 100 times, and they would make *Tasbīḥ* 100 times.' 'And what did you say to them?' asked 'Abdullāh ibn Mas'ūd (ﷺ).' 'I didn't say anything, for I wished to wait and first learn your view on the matter or receive your command.' He (ﷺ) said, 'Would that you ordered them to count their sins...' He (ﷺ) went and we accompanied him until we reached one of those

gatherings. 'Abdullāh ibn Mas'ūd (&) stood over them and said, 'What is this that I see you doing?' They said, 'O Abū 'Abdullāh (i.e. 'Abdullāh ibn Mas'ūd (&)), we are using these pebbles to count the number of times we make *Takbīr*, *Tahlīl*, and *Tasbīh*.' He (&) said, 'Then count your sins... Woe unto you, O Nation of Muhammad, how quickly has come your destruction! These are the companions of Prophet (&) in sufficient numbers, this is his garment that has not yet become tattered, and this is his dish that has not yet broken (i.e., so recent is it that the Prophet (&) died and you are already upon misguidance). By the One Who has my soul in His Hand, you are either upon a Religion that contains more guidance than the Religion of Muhammad, or you are openers of the door of misguidance.' They said, 'By Allāh, O 'Abdur-Rahmān, we intended only to do good!' He (&) said, 'And how many are those who intend to do good, but do not achieve that goal! Indeed, the Messenger of Allāh (&) spoke to us, saying that a group of people recites the Qur'ān, yet it does not go past their collarbones. By Allāh, I do not know, but perhaps most of them are from you.' He then turned away, leaving them.

'Amr ibn Salamah said, "We saw that most participants of those gatherings did battle with us on the day of al-Nahrawān with the Khawārij."[32] What seemed to that group a small issue was in fact grave because they were remembering Allāh (&) in a way that is not legislated in the Qur'ān or Sunnah, and thus they were led to an evil end result, i.e., they ended up fighting the Muslims on the Day of *Nahrawān* with the *Khawārij*. Thus did they part from the way of the believers, in the beginning in how they made *al-Tasbīh*, *al-Tahlīl*, and *al-Takbīr* – while they claimed that all they wanted

---

[32] Related by al-Dārimī (1/68), and its chain is authentic, for all of its narrators are trustworthy. Refer to *Al-Radd 'Ala al-Ta'aqqub al-Hathīth* (pg. 47), written by our Shaykh, Al-Albānī – may Allāh have mercy on him.

was to do good – and later on in fighting against the Muslims – in which case they might also have been deluded into thinking that they were doing good.

In the Final Command of His, the Prophet (ﷺ) Forbade us From One Matter Only: Innovation

If one were to reflect on the words of the Prophet's farewell commands, one would find that the orders to do outnumber the prohibitions, which is accounted for by the fact that if one adheres to the Sunnah, he needs not the details about the paths of misguidance. The commands to do are as follows:

1) Fear Allāh much.
2) Listen and obey.
3) Adhere to the Sunnah of the Prophet (ﷺ) and the Sunnah of the rightly-guided *Khalīfahs*.

As to prohibitions, the Prophet (ﷺ) here only forbade us from one matter, saying, "Beware and stay away from innovated matters," which in a sense signifies: stay away from new and innovated matters, and as a result, you will be saved and become successful. Innovation is the secret that lies behind misguidance, deviance, and utter loss, for it leads to, and sometimes involves, *shirk* (associating partners with Allāh) and disbelief. Therefore whoever closes the door to innovation has become guided, with the permission of Allāh (ﷻ). In regards to innovation, one does well to heed this ḥadīth:

إِنّ الله احتجزَ التوبة عن صاحب كلّ بدعة.

"Indeed, Allāh (ﷻ) prevents the repentance of the possessor of every innovation."[33]

---

[33] Related by Abū al-Shaykh, in "*Al-Tārīkh Aṣbahān*," and Al-Ṭabarānī in "*Al-Awsaṭ*," as well as others. Refer to "*al-Ṣaḥīḥah* (1620)."

Conclusion

Indeed, the Prophet's final commands were similar to his sermons: they caused hearts to quake and eyes to shed tears, but only living hearts and sincere eyes. Hearts quake because of the humiliation we are experiencing in comparison to the honour that we heard of. Eyes shed tears because of the scattering of Muslims and because of division among their ranks, which has befallen us after a period of glory, honour, and dominance.

Yet there is hope: those final commands contain in them that which can save us from the said predicament we find ourselves to be in. Fear of Allāh (ﷻ); war on desires; adherence to the Prophet's Sunnah and Sunnah of the rightly-guided *Khalīfahs*; a correct understanding of the Qur'ān and Sunnah, which corresponds to the understanding of the Companions; and staying aloof from innovations – all of these are contained in the Prophet's final commands. Adhere to those commands and bite on to them with your molars (may Allāh have mercy on you) so that you may be from those who are saved, those who are successful, by the will of Allāh (ﷻ).